FOOD LOVERS

VEGETARIAN

RECIPES SELECTED BY RENE CHAN

Trans
Atlantic
Press

All recipes serve four people, unless otherwise indicated.

For best results when cooking the recipes in this book, buy fresh ingredients and follow the instructions carefully. Make sure that everything is properly cooked through before serving and note that as a general rule vulnerable groups such as the very young, elderly people, pregnant women, convalescents and anyone suffering from an illness should avoid dishes that contain raw or lightly cooked eggs.

For all recipes, quantities are given in metric measures, followed by the standard U.S. cups and imperial measures equivalent. Follow one set or the other, but not a mixture of both because conversions may not be exact. Standard spoon and cup measurements are level and are based on the following:

1 tsp = 5 ml, 1 tbsp = 15 ml, 1 cup = 250 ml / 8 fl oz.

Note that Australian standard tablespoons are 20 ml, so Australian readers should use 3 tsp. in place of 1 tbsp. when measuring small quantities.

The electric oven temperatures in this book are given for conventional ovens with top and bottom heat. When using a fan oven, the temperature should be decreased by about 20–40ºF / 10–20ºC – check the oven manufacturer's instruction book for further guidance. The cooking times given should be used as an approximate guideline only.

Although the recipes in this book are believed to be accurate and true at the time of going to press, neither the authors nor the publisher can accept any legal responsibility or liability for any errors or omissions that may be made nor for any inaccuracies nor for any harm or injury that may come about from following instructions or advice given in this book.

FOOD LOVERS
VEGETARIAN

CONTENTS

SPAGHETTI WITH PEAS AND CHERRY TOMATOES

Ingredients

3 tbsp olive oil

1 garlic clove, finely chopped

2 tbsp fresh basil leaves, chopped

2 tbsp fresh chervil leaves, finely chopped

575 g / 1¼ lb cherry tomatoes, rinsed

450 g / 1 lb spaghetti

150 g / 1 cup frozen peas

Salt and freshly ground pepper

Chervil, to garnish

For the sauce:

2 garlic cloves, peeled and finely chopped

1 tbsp butter

1 splash dry white wine

200 g / 1 cup cream cheese

About 100 ml / ½ cup whipping cream

Salt and freshly ground pepper

Method

Prep and cook time: 30 min

1 Mix together the oil, garlic, basil and chervil.

2 Toss the tomatoes in the herb oil, season with salt and pepper and cook in a skillet over a medium heat for about 4 minutes until just beginning to soften and split.

3 Cook the spaghetti in plenty of boiling salted water until al dente, adding the peas 3 minutes before the end of cooking.

4 To make the sauce, fry the garlic in hot butter, add the white wine and reduce slightly.

5 Stir in the cream cheese and cream, bring to a boil and season with salt and pepper.

6 Drain the pasta and peas and divide between the 4 plates. Pour the sauce over the pasta, arrange the herby tomatoes on top and garnish with chervil.

STUFFED PEPPERS

Ingredients

3 tbsp olive oil

200 g / 1 cup cooked rice

100 g / ¼ lb cherry tomatoes, halved

1 carrot, peeled and coarsely grated

100 g / 1 cup feta cheese, crumbled

2 tbsp freshly chopped basil

4 red (bell) peppers, halved lengthwise
and deseeded

About 100 g / 2 cups white bread
crumbs

Salt and freshly ground pepper

Method

Prep and cook time: 50 min

1 Preheat the oven to 180C (375F / Gas Mark 5).

2 Grease a baking dish with 1 tbsp of oil.

3 Place the rice in a large bowl. Mix in the tomatoes, carrot, crumbled feta and basil and season with salt and pepper.

4 Spoon the filling into the pepper halves and place in the baking dish. Scatter with bread crumbs, drizzle with the remaining oil and bake in the preheated oven for 30 minutes until golden brown.

TOMATO SOUP WITH VEGETABLES

Ingredients

2 carrots, finely chopped

1 celery stalk, sliced

4 tbsp olive oil

2 cloves garlic, finely chopped

4 scallions (spring onions), finely chopped

100 g / ¼ lb string beans (runner beans), topped and tailed and chopped

2 small zucchini (courgettes), finely chopped

400 g / 2 cups canned tomatoes, chopped

875 ml / 3½ cups vegetable broth (stock)

1 bay leaf

1 sprig thyme

1 tbsp tomato paste (purée)

100 g / ½ cup canned chick peas, rinsed and drained

Salt and freshly ground pepper

30 g / ⅓ cup freshly shaved hard cheese, to serve

A few fresh basil leaves, to garnish

Method

Prep and cook time: 50 min

1 Fry the carrots and celery in hot olive oil for about 3 minutes, add the garlic, scallions (spring onions), string beans (runner beans), zucchini (courgette) and tomatoes and continue frying for a further 1–2 minutes.

2 Add the broth (stock), bay leaf and thyme, season with salt and pepper and stir in the tomato paste (purée). Simmer gently for a further 10–15 minutes.

3 Add the chick peas and simmer for 5 minutes until heated through.

4 To serve, ladle into bowls, scatter with hard cheese and garnish with basil leaves.

RICE NOODLES WITH CABBAGE AND RED COCONUT SAUCE

Ingredients

1 shallot, finely chopped

2 garlic cloves, finely chopped

1 tbsp sesame oil

½ tsp chili powder

½ tsp curcuma (turmeric)

½ tsp ground paprika

½ tsp ground five-spice powder

200 ml / generous ¾ cup coconut milk

2 tbsp lime juice

125 ml / ½ cup vegetable broth (stock)

450 g / 1 lb savoy cabbage, chopped into strips or torn into bite-size pieces

50 g / ½ cup soybean shoots

225 g / ½ lb rice noodles

Salt

Method

Prep and cook time: 30 min

1 Fry the shallot and garlic in sesame oil.

2 Add the chili powder, curcuma (turmeric), paprika and five-spice powder and fry briefly then add the coconut milk, lime juice and vegetable broth (stock). Simmer gently for about 5 minutes and season with salt.

3 Add the savoy cabbage and simmer gently for a further 5–7 minutes. Last of all, add the soybean shoots and warm through for 1–2 minutes.

4 Cook the rice noodles in plenty of water according to the package instructions and drain.

5 Divide the noodles between four bowls and top with the savoy cabbage in coconut sauce.

LENTIL AND PEPPER SALAD

Ingredients

300 g / 1½ cups black beluga lentils
(use puy lentils if not available) ,
soaked in water overnight and drained

4 red bell peppers, deseeded
and halved

3 tbsp olive oil

2 garlic cloves, finely chopped

2 tbsp balsamic vinegar

Small handful arugula (rocket), rinsed
and dried

20 g / ¼ cup hard cheese shavings

Salt and freshly ground pepper

Method

Prep and cook time: 1 hour
plus 12 hours soaking time

1 Preheat the oven to 220C (400F / Gas Mark 6).

2 Boil the lentils until soft (about 40 minutes)
and drain.

3 Lay the bell peppers skin side up on a cookie
sheet lined with baking parchment and bake for
about 10 minutes until the skin begins to blister and
turn black.

4 Remove the peppers from the oven, cover with
a damp dish towel and let cool. Once cooled, peel
the skin off the peppers.

5 Chop the peppers into slices, heat the oil in a
skillet and fry the pepper strips.

6 Add the garlic and continue frying for a few
minutes. Season with salt and pepper then remove
from the heat and let cool slightly.

7 Stir in the balsamic vinegar and lentils and season
to taste.

8 Arrange the salad on plates, top with arugula
(rocket) and cheese shavings and serve warm.

PUMPKIN CURRY

Ingredients

1 onion, finely chopped

2 cloves garlic, finely chopped

1 celery stalk, finely sliced

2 tbsp olive oil

¼ tsp cumin

¼ tsp curcuma (turmeric)

Walnut-size piece fresh ginger, peeled and grated

1 tbsp tomato paste (purée)

160 ml / ²/₃ cup dry white wine

900 g / 2 lb pumpkin flesh, deseeded and chopped into 2.5 cm / 1 inch chunks

400 g / 2 cups canned tomatoes, chopped

1 tsp ground paprika

Cayenne pepper

200 g / 6 cups fresh spinach leaves, washed and roughly chopped

Salt

Method

Prep and cook time: 50 min

1 Fry the onion, garlic and celery in hot oil until softened.

2 Add the cumin, curcuma (turmeric) and ginger and continue frying for a further minute.

3 Add the tomato paste (purée) and white wine and stir in the pumpkin and tomatoes. Season with salt, paprika and cayenne pepper.

4 Cover and simmer gently for about 25 minutes, stirring occasionally. Add a little water if necessary.

5 Stir in the spinach shortly before serving the curry. Season with salt and serve.

BEAN GOULASH

Ingredients

1 onion, finely chopped

2 garlic cloves, finely chopped

2 celery stalks, finely chopped

2 tbsp olive oil

½ tsp caraway

1 tbsp tomato paste (purée)

1 tbsp spicy ground paprika

150 ml / ⅔ cup red wine

600 ml / 2½ cups vegetable broth(stock)

400 g / 2 cups canned tomatoes, chopped

400 g / 2½ cups canned kidney beans, rinsed and drained

2 red bell peppers, deseeded and finely chopped

1 red onion, finely chopped

Cayenne pepper

4 tbsp sour cream

Parsley, to garnish

Method

Prep and cook time: 40 min

1 Fry the onion, garlic and celery in hot oil.

2 Add the caraway, tomato paste (purée) and paprika and continue frying for a few minutes.

3 Add the red wine and reduce slightly. Add the vegetable broth (stock) and tomatoes and simmer gently for 20 minutes, stirring occasionally.

4 Push the mixture through a sieve, return to the pan and bring to a boil.

5 Add the beans, chopped peppers and chopped red onion and season to taste with salt and cayenne pepper.

6 Rest for a few minutes to allow the flavors to mingle, ladle into bowls and serve with a dollop of sour cream, garnished with parsley and a sprinkling of cayenne pepper

PUNJABI STYLE CHICK PEAS

Ingredients

300 g / ½ cup dried chick peas, soaked overnight and drained

4 shallots, sliced into rings

4 tbsp olive oil

1 garlic clove, sliced

½ tsp cumin

½ tsp ground coriander

1 tsp garam masala

½ tsp curcuma (turmeric)

225 g / ½ lb floury potatoes, peeled and chopped

2 tomatoes, chopped

2 chili peppers

2 tbsp cilantro (fresh coriander), chopped

Cayenne pepper

Salt

Method

Prep and cook time: 2 hours 20 min
plus 12 hours soaking

1 Cover the chick peas with 1¼ liters / 5 cups of water and simmer over a low heat for 1½ hours until soft.

2 Fry the shallots in hot oil until golden brown, and reserve 1 tbsp to garnish.

3 Add the garlic, cumin, ground coriander, garam masala and curcuma (turmeric) to the shallots in the pan and fry briefly.

4 Add the potatoes, drained chick peas and about 100 ml / scant ½ cup of water.

5 Add the tomatoes and chili peppers, cover and simmer gently for about 30 minutes, stirring occasionally. Add a little more water if necessary.

6 Season to taste with salt and cayenne pepper and stir in the chopped cilantro (fresh coriander).

7 Spoon into bowls and serve garnished with the reserved onions.

SPRING ROLLS
WITH RICOTTA AND SWEET CHILI SAUCE

Ingredients

16 sheets frozen filo pastry, about 350 g / ¾ lb in total, separated and thawed

225 g / ½ lb paneer cheese, chopped into cubes

4 tbsp vegetable oil

100 g / ¼ lb spinach

1 red bell pepper, deseeded and chopped

3 scallions (spring onions), chopped

2 cloves garlic, finely chopped

1 green chili pepper, deseeded and finely chopped

½ tsp lemon zest, finely grated

100 g / ½ cup ricotta cheese

Oil, for deep-frying

Salt and freshly ground pepper

For the sauce:

3½ tbsp sugar

1 tbsp tomato paste (purée)

1 tsp salt

1 tbsp rice vinegar

1 red chili pepper, deseeded and very finely chopped

Method
Prep and cook time: 50 min

1 To make the sauce, bring the sugar and about 4 tbsp of water to a boil and simmer until the mixture turns into a clear syrup.

2 Stir in the tomato paste (purée), salt, vinegar and chili and let cool.

3 To make the filling, fry the paneer cubes in 2 tbsp of vegetable oil until golden brown.

4 Wilt the spinach in the remaining oil and continue frying until steamed dry.

5 Mix together the spinach, bell pepper, scallions (spring onions), garlic, chili, paneer, lemon zest and ricotta and season with salt and pepper.

6 Divide the mixture between the sheets of pastry.

7 Fold in the ends of the pastry squares and roll up. Brush the edges with water and press firmly to close.

8 Deep-fry the spring rolls in hot oil for about 5 minutes, a few at a time, until golden brown. Serve with the chili sauce.

CREAMY MUSHROOMS WITH DUMPLINGS

Ingredients

For the mushroom sauce:

1 shallot, finely chopped

1 garlic clove, finely chopped

About 2 tbsp butter

200 ml / scant 1 cup dry white wine

250 ml / 1 cup whipping cream

2 tbsp crème fraîche

1 tbsp freshly chopped parsley, plus some extra to garnish

1 tbsp snipped chives

450 g / 1 lb fresh wild mushrooms, e.g. cep, slippery jack, birch boletus, thoroughly cleaned and roughly chopped or crumbled

Salt and freshly ground pepper

For the dumplings:

1 shallot, finely chopped

1 tbsp butter

250 ml / 1 cup lukewarm milk

450 g / 1 lb stale white bread, crust removed

3 eggs

2 tbsp freshly chopped parsley

Salt and freshly ground pepper

Method

Prep and cook time: 1 hour 10 min

1 For the dumplings, sweat the shallot in hot butter without coloring until translucent.

2 In a large bowl, pour the warm milk over the bread, add the eggs, parsley and shallot, season with salt and pepper and mix well. Leave to stand for about 20 minutes.

3 Form the dough into smooth round dumplings and simmer gently for about 20 minutes in salted water.

4 For the mushroom sauce, sweat the shallot and garlic briefly in hot butter, add the wine and reduce slightly. Add the cream and crème fraîche, simmer until slightly thickened and season with salt and pepper. Add the parsley and chives.

5 Fry the mushrooms in hot butter for 3–4 minutes until golden brown and season with salt and pepper.

6 Arrange the mushrooms on plates, pour over the cream sauce, add the dumplings and serve garnished with parsley.

PANCAKES WITH SPINACH AND MOZZARELLA

Ingredients

For the batter:

150 g / 1½ cups flour

3 eggs

125 ml / ½ cup milk

About 125 ml / ½ cup sparkling mineral water

2 tbsp melted butter

Salt, to taste

Butter, for frying

For the filling:

1 tbsp butter

450 g / 1 lb fresh spinach, rinsed

2 garlic cloves, finely sliced

250 g / 1¼ cups mozzarella cheese, drained and sliced

50 g / ½ cup pine nuts, toasted without fat

Cherry tomatoes, to garnish

Fresh herbs, e.g. sage, tarragon, to garnish

Method

Prep and cook time: 25 min plus 20 min resting time

1 Preheat the oven to 200C (400F / Gas Mark 6).

2 To make the batter, beat together all the ingredients and rest for 20 minutes. If the batter is too thick, add a little more water.

3 Heat a little butter in a skillet and make 8–12 thin pancakes from the batter. Set aside and keep warm.

4 To make the filling, melt the butter in a clean pan and fry the spinach and garlic until the spinach has wilted.

5 Divide the spinach between the pancakes, top with the cheese and fold the pancakes into quarters.

6 Place the pancakes on a cookie sheet lined with baking parchment, cover with foil and bake in the oven for about 5 minutes, until the cheese has melted.

7 Arrange the pancakes on a warmed plate and serve garnished with tomatoes and herbs.

MUSHROOM TAGLIATELLE

Ingredients

350 g / ¾ lb tagliatelle

450 g / 1 lb mixed mushrooms, e. g. mu err, cep, chestnut mushrooms, well cleaned and chopped

4 tbsp olive oil

1 zucchini (courgette), washed and chopped

2 garlic cloves, peeled and finely chopped

Salt and freshly ground pepper

1 tbsp freshly chopped parsley, to garnish

Method

Prep and cook time: 30 min

1 Cook the tagliatelle in salted water until al dente.

2 In a large skillet, fry the mushrooms in hot oil for about 3 minutes.

3 Add the zucchini (courgette) and garlic and continue frying for 1–2 minutes.

4 Toss the mushroom mixture with the pasta, season with salt and pepper, scatter with parsley and arrange on plates.

ROMANIAN BEAN STEW

Ingredients

200 g / 1 cup dried navy (haricot) beans, soaked overnight and drained

2 onions, finely chopped

1 garlic clove, finely chopped

100 g / ½ cup vegetarian sausage or vegetarian bacon, finely chopped

1 tbsp olive oil

225 g / ½ lb string (green) beans, halved

625 ml / 2½ cups vegetable broth (stock)

2 sprigs fresh savory, leaves plucked

Salt and freshly ground pepper

Fresh herbs, to garnish

Method

Prep and cook time: 50 min

1 Cook the beans in a large pan of salted water over a low heat for about 30 minutes until soft.

2 Fry the onions, garlic and vegetarian sausage or vegetarian bacon in hot oil for 1–2 minutes, add the string (green) beans and vegetable broth (stock), cover and simmer for about 8 minutes.

3 Stir in the drained navy (haricot) beans and savory leaves and season to taste with salt and pepper.

STIR-FRY WITH TOFU

Ingredients

225 g / ½ lb tofu, chopped into
2 cm / ¾ inch cubes

1 onion, finely chopped

3 tbsp vegetable oil

450 g / 1 lb broccoli, separated
into florets

2 red (bell) peppers, chopped
into strips

1 garlic clove, finely chopped

50 g / ⅓ cup cashew nuts

100 g / 1 cup bean sprouts

Light soy sauce

Salt and freshly ground pepper

Method

Prep and cook time: 20 min

1 Fry the tofu and onion in hot oil in a skillet or
wok for 1–2 minutes.

2 Add the broccoli and pepper strips and continue
to fry for a further 2–3 minutes, stirring occasionally.

3 At the end of cooking time add the garlic,
cashew nuts and bean sprouts and fry for a further
2–3 minutes until cooked.

4 Season with soy sauce, salt and pepper to serve.

SPINACH QUICHE

Ingredients

For a tart pan (tin) 26 cm / 10 inch diameter

For the pastry:

200 g / 2 cups flour

¼ tsp salt

100 g / ½ cup butter, cold, chopped, plus extra for greasing

1 egg

For the filling:

2 tbsp butter

1 leek, finely chopped

2 garlic cloves, finely chopped

400 g / 1¾ cups cream cheese

3 eggs

250 ml / 1 cup whipping cream

100 g / 1 cup freshly grated hard cheese

450 g / 1 lb young spinach, rinsed and roughly chopped

Nutmeg

Salt and freshly ground pepper

Method

Prep and cook time: 1 hour
plus 30 min chilling time

1 Preheat the oven to 200C (400F / Gas Mark 6).

2 Pour the flour onto a work surface in a heap and add the salt. Make a well in the middle and scatter with the butter.

3 Crack the egg into the well, add 2–3 tbsp of lukewarm water and cut all ingredients together with a knife to form a crumbly consistency.

4 Using your hands, knead quickly to a dough, form into a ball, wrap in plastic wrap (cling film) and chill for around 30 minutes.

5 To make the filling, melt the butter in a pan and gently fry the leek and garlic until soft.

6 Mix the cream cheese with the eggs, cream and half the hard cheese to a smooth consistency.

7 Add the spinach, garlic and leek and season with salt, pepper and nutmeg.

8 Roll the pastry out between two sheets of plastic wrap and use to line a greased tart pan.

9 Pour the filling into the pastry case and smooth the surface. Sprinkle with the remaining hard cheese and bake for around 40 minutes until golden brown.

LENTIL AND POTATO CURRY

Ingredients

1 onion, finely chopped

2 garlic cloves, finely chopped

Walnut-size piece fresh ginger, peeled and grated

1 tsp curcuma (turmeric)

½ tsp cayenne pepper

½ tsp ground coriander

½ tsp cumin

2 tsp ghee or clarified butter

450 g / 1 lb waxy potatoes, roughly chopped

225 g / ½ lb pumpkin flesh, roughly chopped

250 g / 1¼ cups lentils, rinsed and drained

250 g / 1¼ cups canned tomatoes, chopped

Salt

2 tbsp cilantro (fresh coriander), to garnish

Method

Prep and cook time: 50 min

1 Sweat the onion and garlic with the ginger, curcuma (turmeric), cayenne pepper, coriander and cumin in hot ghee for 4–5 minutes, stirring occasionally.

2 Add the potatoes, pumpkin, lentils, tomatoes and just enough water to cover all the ingredients. Cover and simmer gently for 30–40 minutes, stirring occasionally.

3 Season with salt and serve garnished with cilantro (fresh coriander) leaves.

STIR-FRIED TOFU
AND SNOW PEAS
WITH NOODLES

Ingredients

350 g / ¾ lb egg noodles

450 g / 1 lb tofu, cubed

1 onion, finely chopped

2 tbsp sesame oil

100 g / ¼ lb snow peas (sugar snaps),
halved

100 g / ½ cup canned corn
(sweetcorn) kernels, drained

100 g / 1 cup bean spouts

2 garlic cloves, finely chopped

2 tbsp soy sauce

Salt

Method
Prep and cook time: 20 min

1 Cook the noodles according to the package
instructions.

2 In a wok or large skillet, stir-fry the tofu and onion
in hot oil for 2 minutes.

3 Add the snow peas (sugar snaps), corn
(sweetcorn), bean sprouts, garlic and soy sauce and
continue cooking for a further 4 minutes, stirring
occasionally.

4 Toss the stir-fry with the noodles and season to
taste with salt.

ROASTED VEGETABLES

Ingredients

2 fennel bulbs, halved, core removed and chopped into strips

2 red (bell) peppers, deseeded and chopped into large pieces

4 red onions, chopped into segments

1 leek, chopped into thick rings

4 tbsp olive oil

2 tbsp rosemary leaves

Salt and freshly ground pepper

Method

Prep and cook time: 45 min

1 Preheat the oven to 200C (400F / Gas Mark 6).

2 Place all the vegetables in an ovenproof dish and drizzle with olive oil.

3 Scatter with rosemary, season with salt and pepper and bake in the preheated oven for about 30 minutes, turning the vegetables occasionally.

MINI CHEESE SOUFFLÉS

Ingredients

For 4 ramekins, each
approx 250 ml / 1 cup

Butter, for greasing

Bread crumbs

75 g / 6 tbsp butter

4 eggs, separated

1 tbsp freshly chopped parsley

2½ tsp freshly grated nutmeg

150 g / 1½ cups freshly grated cheese
(e.g. Emmental, Cheddar)

4 tbsp whipping cream

2 tbsp crème fraîche

2 tbsp flour

Salt

Method

Prep and cook time: 30 min

1 Preheat the oven to 200C (400F / Gas Mark 6).

2 Grease 4 ovenproof ramekins with melted butter and scatter with bread crumbs.

3 Beat the butter, egg yolks, parsley and nutmeg until creamy.

4 Stir in small amounts of the cheese, cream and crème fraîche until everything is well combined.

5 Beat the egg whites until stiff and fold into the cheese mixture along with the flour and season with a pinch of salt.

6 Pour into the ramekins and bake in the preheated oven for about 15 minutes until golden brown. Serve immediately.

SPICY BEAN BURGERS

Ingredients

2 scallions (spring onions)

450 g / 1 lb fava (broad) beans

2 tbsp soy sauce

1 egg

2 tbsp bread crumbs

2 tbsp parsley, chopped

2 tbsp grated hard cheese

2 tbsp olive oil

Salt and freshly ground pepper

In addition:

200 g / 1 cup yogurt

1 tbsp whipping cream

1 tbsp lemon juice

Salt and freshly ground pepper

1 large red bell pepper, deseeded and diced, to serve

Parsley, to garnish

Method

Prep and cook time: 30 min

1 Wash, trim and finely chop the scallions (spring onions).

2 Simmer the beans for about 5 minutes in salted water, then drain and purée.

3 Put the beans into a bowl with the scallions, soy sauce, egg, bread crumbs, parsley and cheese and mix well until thoroughly combined. Season to taste with pepper.

4 Shape the mixture into 8 flattish burgers. Heat the oil in a large skillet and fry the burgers for about 2–3 minutes each side, or until golden brown.

5 Mix the yogurt with the cream, lemon juice, parsley, salt and pepper.

6 Serve the burgers on plates with yogurt, scatter with diced red pepper and garnish with parsley.

CAULIFLOWER GRATIN

Ingredients

Butter, for greasing

800 g / 3 cups cauliflower florets, rinsed

100 ml / scant ½ cup whipping cream

100 ml / scant ½ cup milk

60 g / ⅔ cup Emmental cheese, grated

2 eggs

Nutmeg

2 slices white bread, crusts removed, chopped

Salt and freshly ground pepper

Method

Prep and cook time: 40 min

1 Preheat the oven to 200C (400F / Gas Mark 6).

2 Grease an ovenproof dish or pan with butter.

3 Blanch the cauliflower florets in boiling salted water for about 2 minutes. Drain, refresh in cold water, drain again and place in the greased dish.

4 Whisk together the cream, milk, cheese and eggs, season with salt, pepper and nutmeg and pour over the cauliflower.

5 Scatter the bread over the cauliflower and bake in the preheated oven for about 25 minutes.

LENTIL LOAF WITH VEGETABLES

Ingredients

1 tbsp olive oil

2 tbsp sunflower seeds

100 g / ½ cup dry yellow lentils, rinsed

225 g / ½ lb floury potatoes, coarsely grated

2 onions, chopped

1 clove garlic, chopped

1 leek, chopped

100 g / ¼ lb white turnips, chopped

100 g / ⅔ cup pistachio nuts, chopped

2–3 tbsp whole wheat flour

2 eggs

2 tbsp freshly chopped parsley

Nutmeg

Salt and freshly ground pepper

Freshly cooked vegetables, to serve

Method

Prep and cook time: 1 hour 20 min

1 Preheat the oven to 180C (325F / Gas Mark 3).

2 Grease a loaf pan with oil and scatter with sunflower seeds.

3 Place the lentils in a saucepan and cover with cold water. Bring to a boil, cover and simmer for about 30 minutes until cooked but not disintegrating. Drain and let cool.

4 If the potatoes are very wet, squeeze to remove excess liquid. Place in a mixing bowl.

5 Add the onions, garlic, leek, turnip, pistachios, flour, eggs, lentils and parsley to the potatoes and mix well.

6 Season the mixture with salt, pepper and nutmeg and turn into the loaf pan. Smooth the surface and bake for 40 minutes until golden brown. Turn the loaf out of the pan, slice and arrange with freshly cooked vegetables.

ORZO SALAD WITH FETA

Ingredients

450 g / 1 lb orzo (rice-shaped pasta)

2 shallots, peeled and finely chopped

3 tbsp olive oil

2 red bell peppers, deseeded and roughly chopped

2 yellow bell peppers, deseeded and roughly chopped

450 g / 1 lb asparagus, chopped diagonally into 2.5 cm / 1 inch pieces

1 tsp tomato paste (purée)

About 125 ml / ½ cup vegetable broth (stock)

Zest and juice of ½ lemon

1 tbsp freshly chopped basil

100 g / 1 cup feta cheese

2 tbsp chopped pine nuts, toasted in a skillet

Salt and freshly ground pepper

Fresh lettuce leaves, to serve (optional)

Method

Prep and cook time: 30 min

1 Cook the pasta in plenty of salted water according to the package instructions until al dente.

2 Sweat the shallots in hot oil, add the peppers and asparagus and continue frying for a few minutes.

3 Stir in the tomato paste (purée) and vegetable broth (stock) and simmer for about 4 minutes, until the vegetables are cooked but still firm and the liquid has almost completely evaporated.

4 Stir in the lemon zest, basil and drained pasta and toss well. Season to taste with lemon juice, salt and pepper.

5 Crumble the feta over the pasta, scatter with pine nuts, arrange on plates and serve with salad leaves (optional).

GNOCCHI WITH VEGETARIAN SAUSAGE

Ingredients

For the gnocchi:

900 g / 2 lb floury potatoes

200 g / 2 cups flour, plus extra for kneading and rolling

1 egg

1 tsp salt

For the sauce:

6 vegetarian sausages, chopped

1 shallot, finely chopped

2 cloves garlic, finely chopped

2 tbsp olive oil

600 g / 3 cups canned tomatoes, chopped

2 sprigs basil

4 tbsp hard cheese, freshly grated

Salt and freshly ground pepper

Method

Prep and cook time: 1 hour 15 min

1 To make the gnocchi, cook the potatoes in salted water for about 30 minutes until soft, then drain. Peel the potatoes, press through a potato ricer and leave to steam dry.

2 Mix the potatoes with the flour, egg and salt and knead to a dough which leaves the bowl clean, adding a little more flour if the dough is too sticky. Cover and rest for about 15 minutes.

3 On a floured surface, form the dough into long rolls and chop off slices 2 cm / ¾ inch thick. Form the gnocchi by rolling each slice against the tines of a fork. Cover and leave to rest on the floured surface.

4 To make the sauce, sweat the sausages, shallot and garlic in hot oil. Add the tomatoes and simmer gently for 10 minutes, stirring occasionally.

5 Pluck a few basil leaves and reserve for the garnish. Chop the remainder roughly and add to the sauce. Season the sauce with salt and pepper.

6 Simmer the gnocchi in salted water for about 5 minutes.

7 Drain the gnocchi and arrange on plates. Pour over the sauce and scatter with hard cheese. Serve garnished with the reserved basil leaves.

TABBOULEH

Ingredients

400 ml / 1 ⅔ cups vegetable broth (stock)

200 g / ¾ cup bulgur wheat

2 tomatoes

2 chili peppers, deseeded and finely chopped

4 scallions (spring onions), chopped into rings

1 zucchini (courgette), finely chopped

1 celery stalk, finely chopped

40 g / 2 cups fresh parsley, roughly chopped

3 tbsp lemon juice

4 tbsp olive oil

Salt and freshly ground pepper

Parsley sprigs, to garnish

Method

Prep and cook time: 1 hour

1 Heat the broth (stock) in a saucepan, stir in the bulgur and leave for 30 minutes, fluffing up with a fork from time to time.

2 Slit crosses in the skins of the tomatoes. Blanch in boiling water then refresh, peel, halve and deseed. Chop the flesh.

3 Mix the vegetables, parsley, lemon juice and olive oil into the bulgur and season with salt and pepper. Let sit for 10–15 minutes.

4 Before serving, check the seasoning and adjust if necessary with salt and pepper. Garnish with parsley and serve.

LENTIL SHEPHERD'S PIE

Ingredients

350 g / ¾ lb floury potatoes

2 onions, finely chopped

2 tbsp vegetable oil

2 carrots, finely chopped

1 yellow bell pepper, deseeded and chopped

1 red bell pepper, deseeded and chopped

1 tbsp flour

250 ml / 1 cup vegetable broth (stock)

100 g / 1 cup frozen peas, thawed

200 g / 1 cup canned lentils, rinsed and drained

About 75 ml / $^1/_3$ cup hot milk

Nutmeg

Butter, for greasing

50 g / ½ cup grated cheese

Salt and freshly ground pepper

Method

Prep and cook time: 1 hour 30 min

1 Preheat the oven to 190C (375F / Gas Mark 5).

2 Cook the potatoes in boiling salted water for about 25 minutes until soft.

3 Sweat the onions in hot oil, add the carrots and red bell pepper and continue frying.

4 Dust with the flour and add the vegetable broth (stock).

5 Stir in the peas and lentils and season with salt and pepper.

6 Drain and mash the potatoes, stir in the hot milk and season with salt, pepper and nutmeg.

7 Grease 4 individual pie dishes with butter.

8 Spoon the lentil mixture into the dishes, top with mashed potato and scatter with cheese.

9 Bake in the middle of the preheated oven for 25 minutes or until golden brown.

POTATO GRATIN
WITH VEGETABLES

Ingredients

675 g / 1½ lb waxy potatoes

450 g / 1 lb broccoli florets

3 tomatoes, quartered, deseeded and chopped

2 scallions (spring onions), chopped into fine rings

2 garlic cloves, finely chopped

50 g / ½ cup pitted black olives, roughly chopped

½ tsp dried oregano

½ tsp dried thyme

2 tbsp olive oil

250 ml / 1 cup yogurt

2 eggs

50 g / ½ cup grated Emmental cheese

Salt and freshly ground pepper

Method

Prep and cook time: 1 hour 10 min

1 Preheat the oven to 180C (375F / Gas Mark 5).

2 Boil the potatoes for about 25 minutes until cooked through. Drain, let steam dry and chop into slices.

3 Blanch the broccoli florets in salted water for about 3 minutes until al dente. Drain, refresh and drain again.

4 Mix together the tomatoes, scallions (spring onions), garlic, olives, oregano and thyme and season with salt and pepper.

5 Grease an ovenproof dish with 1 tsp olive oil.

6 Lay the potato slices and broccoli florets in the dish in overlapping layers.

7 Beat the yogurt with the eggs and pour over the potatoes.

8 Spread the vegetable mixture over the potatoes, scatter with cheese and bake for about 30 minutes.

SPINACH FRITTATA

Ingredients

450 g / 1 lb potatoes

3 tbsp olive oil

2 scallions (spring onions), washed and trimmed

1 garlic clove, peeled and finely chopped

6 eggs

225 g / ½ lb frozen creamed spinach, thawed

Nutmeg

225 g / ½ lb cherry tomatoes, halved

Salt and freshly ground pepper

Sprouts and herbs, to garnish

Method
Prep and cook time: 50 min

1 Preheat the oven to 160C (325F / Gas Mark 3).

2 Peel and wash the potatoes and cut into about 1½ cm / ½ inch cubes. Cook the diced potatoes in boiling, salted water for about 10 minutes then drain thoroughly.

3 Heat the olive oil in a skillet and sweat the scallions (spring onions) and garlic until translucent.

4 Add the potatoes and briefly fry all together. Transfer the contents of the pan to an ovenproof dish.

5 Whisk the eggs, mix with the thawed spinach, season with salt, pepper and nutmeg and add the mixture to the dish.

6 Arrange the halved cherry tomatoes on top and put into the preheated oven for about 30 minutes or until the egg is set. Cover with foil if it browns too quickly.

7 Take out of the oven, cut into pieces and serve garnished with bean sprouts and herbs.

COUSCOUS WITH PUMPKIN AND CASHEWS

Ingredients

1 small pumpkin, about 1 kg / 2¼ lb, deseeded, peeled and chopped

2–3 tbsp olive oil

1 onion, chopped

1 tsp confectioners' (icing) sugar

1 tsp freshly chopped rosemary

300 g / 1½ cups instant couscous

100 g / ⅔ cup cashew nuts

1 tbsp freshly chopped parsley

½ tsp ground cinnamon

Salt and freshly ground pepper

Method

Prep and cook time: 45 min

1 Blanch the pumpkin flesh in boiling salted water for about 5 minutes until almost cooked through. Drain and leave to steam dry.

2 Heat the oil in a large saucepan and fry the onion and pumpkin for 2–3 minutes until golden brown. Dust with confectioners' (icing) sugar and let caramelize slightly.

3 Season with rosemary, salt and pepper, then add about 375 ml / 1½ cups of water and the couscous. Cover and leave for about 10 minutes until all the water has been absorbed.

4 Stir in the cashew nuts, parsley and cinnamon, season with salt and pepper and serve.

KORMA WITH SAFFRON RICE

Ingredients

250 g / 1¼ cups basmati and wild rice mixture

¼ tsp ground saffron

1 onion, finely chopped

2 tbsp ghee or clarified butter

1 tsp curcuma (turmeric)

½ tsp cumin

½ tsp ground ginger

150 ml / ⅔ cup vegetable broth (stock)

600 g / 2 cups cauliflower florets

100 g / ⅔ cup peeled almonds, roughly chopped

2 carrots, peeled and roughly chopped

200 g / 2 cups canned chick peas, rinsed and drained

150 ml / ⅔ cup yogurt

225 g / ½ lb fresh spinach, rinsed and spun dry

Salt and freshly ground pepper

Method

Prep and cook time: 40 min

1 Cook the rice with the saffron in salted water according to the package instructions.

2 Sweat the onion in hot ghee. Add the curcuma (turmeric), cumin and ginger and continue frying for a few minutes then pour in the vegetable broth (stock).

3 Add the cauliflower, almonds, carrots and chick peas, season with salt, cover and simmer for about 15 minutes, stirring occasionally, until the vegetables are cooked through.

4 Stir in the yogurt and spinach, remove from the heat and season with salt and pepper.

5 Divide the rice between 4 plates and top with the curry.

NOODLES WITH PEANUT SAUCE AND TOFU

Ingredients

For the peanut sauce:

100 g / ½ cup unsalted peanuts, toasted and finely chopped

2 shallots, finely chopped

2 garlic cloves, finely chopped

3 tbsp sweet soy sauce

Juice of ½ lemon

1 tsp chili paste

1 tbsp sugar

2 tbsp groundnut oil

300 ml / 1¼ cups coconut milk

Salt

For the noodles:

450 g / 1 lb oriental wheat flour noodles

225 g / ½ lb red cabbage, chopped into fine strips

1 red bell pepper, deseeded and chopped into strips.

4 scallions (spring onions), chopped into rings

4 carrots, chopped into fine strips

225 g / ½ lb tofu, chopped into cubes

Method
Prep and cook time: 40 min

1 To make the sauce, place the peanuts, shallots, garlic, soy sauce, lemon juice, chili paste and sugar in a tall mixing beaker and purée to a creamy paste using a hand-held blender.

2 Heat the groundnut oil in a pan and briefly fry the peanut paste. Pour in the coconut milk, stir until smooth then simmer for about 3 minutes until slightly thickened. Season with salt.

3 Cook the noodles according to the package instructions. Drain and divide between 4 plates.

4 Spoon the sauce over the noodles, scatter with the red cabbage and pepper strips, scallions (spring onions), carrot strips and tofu, and serve.

ORIENTAL NOODLE BAKE

Ingredients

225 g / ½ lb mie noodles

1 garlic clove, chopped

400 ml / 1²/₃ cups coconut milk

2 tbsp soy sauce

Cayenne pepper

3 eggs

5 g / ¼ oz dried mu err mushrooms, soaked in water according to package instructions

3 tbsp butter

225 g / ½ lb snow peas (mangetout), halved

2 carrots, pared into very thin slices with a peeler

4 scallions (spring onions), chopped into rings

1 red bell pepper, deseeded and finely sliced

2 tbsp chopped cilantro (fresh coriander)

2–3 tbsp bread crumbs

Cilantro (fresh coriander) leaves, to garnish

Method

Prep and cook time: 1 hour

1 Preheat the oven to 200C (400F / Gas Mark 6).

2 Cook the noodles according to the package instructions, refresh and drain.

3 Mix together the garlic and coconut milk, season to taste with some of the soy sauce and some cayenne pepper and stir in the eggs.

4 Drain the mushrooms, pat dry and chop into fine slices.

5 Heat 1 tbsp of butter in a skillet and fry the snow peas (sugar snaps) with 2–3 tbsp of water for 2–3 minutes. Add the carrots and fry for a further 2 minutes.

6 Stir in the scallions (spring onions), bell pepper, mushrooms and chopped cilantro (fresh coriander) and season with soy sauce.

7 Place the noodles into a greased ovenproof dish and spread the vegetable mixture on top.

8 Pour over the coconut sauce, sprinkle with bread crumbs, dot with the remaining butter and bake for about 20 minutes.

9 Garnish with cilantro (fresh coriander) leaves and serve.

POTATO SOUFFLÉS

Ingredients

575 g / 1¼ lb potatoes

Butter, for greasing

225 g / ½ lb filo pastry

1 onion, peeled and finely chopped

50 g / ¼ cup butter

100 g / ½ cup quark

4 sprigs fresh marjoram, leaves stripped and finely chopped

75 g / ¾ cup grated hard cheese

2 eggs, separated

Nutmeg

Salt and freshly ground pepper

Marjoram, to garnish

Method

Prep and cook time: 1 hour 10 min

1 Preheat the oven to 180C (375F / Gas Mark 5).

2 Cook the potatoes in salted boiling water for 30 minutes until soft. Drain, peel and press through a ricer. Leave to steam dry and cool slightly.

3 Grease 4 ramekins with butter.

4 Lay out the filo pastry in double layers and cut out squares about 15×15 cm /6×6 inches. Line the ramekins with the pastry and brush with melted butter.

5 Fry the onion in hot butter until translucent and let cool slightly.

6 Mix the quark with the chopped marjoram, two thirds of the hard cheese, the egg yolks, onion and potatoes.

7 Beat the egg whites until stiff, then fold carefully into the potato mixture and season to taste with salt, pepper and nutmeg.

8 Spoon into the ramekins and scatter with the remaining cheese.

9 Bake for about 25 minutes in the middle of the preheated oven until golden brown. Garnish with marjoram sprigs and serve.

TAGLIATELLE WITH LENTILS AND CAPERS

Ingredients

450 g / 1 lb tagliatelle

1 onion, peeled and finely chopped

2 garlic cloves, peeled and finely chopped

1 celery stalk, washed and sliced

3 tbsp olive oil

100 g / ½ cup red lentils

About 150 ml / ⅔ cup vegetable broth (stock)

1 zucchini (courgette), washed and finely chopped

1 tbsp capers

Salt and freshly ground pepper

Grated hard cheese, to serve (optional)

Method

Prep and cook time: 25 min

1 Cook the tagliatelle in salted water until al dente and drain.

2 Fry the onion, garlic and celery in hot oil until softened.

3 Add the lentils and broth (stock) to the onion and simmer for about 5 minutes.

4 Add the chopped zucchini (courgette) and simmer for a further 5 minutes until the zucchini is cooked through.

5 Add the capers, toss the sauce and noodles until thoroughly combined and season with salt and pepper. Serve with grated hard cheese (optional).

GREEN PEA SOUP

Ingredients

1 shallot, finely chopped

1 garlic clove, finely chopped

1 tbsp butter

400 g / 3 cups frozen peas, thawed

Walnut-size piece fresh ginger, peeled and grated

About 625 ml / 2½ cups vegetable broth (stock)

100 g / ¼ lb floury potatoes, peeled and finely grated

1 sprig fresh basil, leaves finely chopped

4 tbsp crème fraîche

Salt and freshly ground pepper

2 tbsp pumpkinseed oil (optional, to serve)

Method

Prep and cook time: 30 min

1 Sweat the shallot and garlic in hot butter until softened.

2 Add the peas, ginger and broth (stock) and bring to a boil.

3 Add the grated potatoes and simmer gently for about 15 minutes.

4 Add the basil and crème fraîche to the soup and purée until smooth (the purée can be pushed through a sieve to give an even smoother texture).

5 Reduce to the desired thickness with more broth if necessary and season with salt and pepper.

6 To serve, ladle into bowls, drizzle with pumpkinseed oil and pull the tip of a spoon through the oil to give a marbled effect.

CONCHIGLIE WITH TOMATOES AND MOZZARELLA

Ingredients

350 g / ¾ lb large conchiglie pasta shells

3 tbsp olive oil

2 shallots, finely chopped

2 cloves garlic, finely chopped

1 celery stalk, finely chopped

1 splash dry white wine

400 g / 2 cups canned tomatoes, chopped

300 g / 10 oz mozzarella cheese, finely chopped

1 tbsp freshly chopped parsley

Salt and cayenne pepper

Hard cheese, to serve (optional)

Parsley, to garnish

Method

Prep and cook time: 50 min

1 Preheat the oven to 180C (375F / Gas Mark 5).

2 Cook the conchiglie in boiling salted water until al dente. Refresh under cold running water and let drain.

3 Grease an ovenproof dish with a little oil.

4 Sweat the shallots, garlic and celery in the remaining oil.

5 Add the white wine and tomatoes, simmer for about 5 minutes, remove from the heat and season with salt and cayenne pepper.

6 Fill the conchiglie with the tomato sauce and place in the ovenproof dish, spooning any leftover sauce into the spaces between the conchiglie.

7 Scatter the mozzarella over the conchiglie and bake in the preheated oven for about 20 minutes.

8 Remove from the oven and garnish with parsley. Serve with hard cheese (optional).

POTATO GRATIN

Ingredients

150 g / ¾ cup quark

150 g / ¾ cup cream cheese

3 egg whites, beaten until stiff

2 tbsp freshly chopped parsley

450 g / 1 lb waxy potatoes, peeled and chopped into 1 cm / ½ inch cubes

450 g / 1 lb kohlrabi, peeled and chopped into 1 cm / ½ inch cubes

225 g / ½ lb snow peas (sugar snaps), halved

225 g / ½ lb mozzarella cheese, sliced

Salt and freshly ground pepper

Method

Prep and cook time: 1 hour

1 Preheat the oven to 180C (375F / Gas Mark 5).

2 Beat the quark and cream cheese together until smooth.

3 Fold the beaten egg whites, parsley and vegetables into the quark mixture and season with salt and pepper.

4 Spoon the mixture into an ovenproof dish, lay the mozzarella slices on top and bake in the preheated oven for about 40 minutes. Cover with foil if the gratin colors too quickly.

SPICY STIR-FRIED VEGETABLES

Ingredients

4 tbsp sesame oil

2 garlic cloves, chopped

1 tbsp peeled and chopped
fresh ginger

2 shallots, peeled and finely chopped

450 g / 1 lb broccoli, separated
into florets

2 carrots, chopped into 5 cm / 2 inch
strips

225 g / ½ lb pak choi, rinsed, drained
and chopped into 2 cm / ¾ inch strips

2 scallions (spring onions), chopped
into fine rings

½ tsp ground five-spice powder

¼ tsp cayenne pepper

½ tsp corn starch (cornflour)

3 tbsp soy sauce

4 tbsp vegetable broth (stock)

½ tsp sambal oelek (chili paste)

Method

Prep and cook time: 30 min

1 Heat the oil in a wok or large skillet. Fry the
garlic, ginger and shallots for a few minutes.

2 Add the broccoli and carrots and continue to stir-
fry for about 6 minutes.

3 Add the pak choi and scallions (spring onions)
and fry for a further 1–2 minutes, then season with
five-spice powder and cayenne pepper.

4 Mix the corn starch (cornflour) to a smooth paste
with the soy sauce, vegetable broth (stock) and
sambal oelek (chili paste). Stir into the vegetables,
cover and cook for a further 1–2 minutes.

MINI QUICHES
WITH MUSHROOMS

Ingredients

For 12 quiches or for 1 muffin pan

Butter for greasing

Bread crumbs

2–3 tbsp clarified butter

1 onion, finely chopped

1 garlic clove, finely chopped

225 g / ½ lb white mushrooms, chopped

100 g / ¼ lb oyster mushrooms, chopped

200 g / ½ cup cep mushrooms, chopped

350 g / 1¾ cups quark

200 g / 7 oz mozzarella cheese, finely chopped

4 eggs

3–4 tbsp cream of wheat (semolina) or fine oatmeal

50 g / ½ cup chopped pine nuts

Salt and freshly ground pepper

Garnish:

Fresh basil, chopped into strips

2–3 tbsp pine nuts

Method

Prep and cook time: 1 hour

1 Preheat the oven to 200C (400F, Gas / Mark 6).

2 Grease a muffin pan with butter and scatter with bread crumbs.

3 Heat the clarified butter in a pan and sweat the onions and garlic until translucent.

4 Turn up the heat, add the mushrooms and fry for a few minutes.

5 Turn the heat back down, season lightly with salt and pepper and continue frying until all the liquid has evaporated.

6 Beat together the quark, mozzarella, eggs, cream of wheat and pine nuts until smooth and season with salt and pepper.

7 Drain the mushrooms if necessary and add to the quark mixture.

8 Spoon the mixture into the muffin pan and bake in the preheated oven for about 20 minutes until golden brown.

9 Remove from the oven, let cool for 5 minutes then remove carefully from the muffin pan.

10 Serve warm or cold, garnished with basil and pine nuts.

MIXED BEANS WITH POTATOES

Ingredients

200 g / 1 cup dried cannellini beans, soaked overnight and drained

100 g / ½ cup dried chick peas, soaked overnight and drained

1 shallot, finely chopped

2 garlic cloves, finely chopped

1 red chili pepper, deseeded and finely chopped

2 tbsp olive oil

150 g / ¾ cup canned tomatoes, chopped

About 150 ml / ²/₃ cup vegetable broth (stock)

450 g / 1 lb waxy potatoes, peeled and chopped into bite-size chunks

Salt and freshly ground pepper

Fresh cilantro (coriander) leaves, to garnish

Method

Prep and cook time: 1 hour plus 12 hours soaking

1 Bring the beans and chick peas to a boil in a large pan of salted water, cover and simmer for about 45 minutes until cooked through.

2 Sweat the shallots, garlic and chili in hot oil.

3 Add the tomatoes, vegetable broth (stock) and potatoes, season with salt and pepper and simmer for about 20 minutes, stirring occasionally. If the mixture becomes too dry, add a little more vegetable broth.

4 Stir in the drained beans and chick peas, season to taste with salt and pepper and serve garnished with cilantro (coriander) leaves.

CHEESE AND VEGETABLE PIE

Ingredients

For 1 pie dish; 26 cm / 10 inch diameter

450 g / 1 lb puff pastry, thawed if frozen

2 tbsp olive oil, plus extra for greasing

50 g / ½ cup freshly grated hard cheese

4 tomatoes, rinsed, cored and chopped or 200 g / 1 cup chopped canned tomatoes

450 g / 1 lb pumpkin flesh, peeled and chopped into cubes

450 g / 1 lb floury potatoes, peeled and chopped into cubes

2 zucchini (courgettes), rinsed, cleaned and sliced

1 onion, finely chopped

2 garlic cloves, finely chopped

50 g / ½ cup black olives, pitted and sliced

1 tsp dried thyme

4 tbsp white bread crumbs

200 g / 7 oz feta cheese

150 g / 5 oz mozzarella cheese, sliced

2 tbsp freshly chopped parsley

Salt and freshly ground pepper

Lettuce leaves, to serve

Method

Prep and cook time: 1 hour 20 min

1 Preheat the oven to 180C (375F / Gas Mark 5).

2 Roll out the pastry and cut out two circles for the base and lid of the pie.

3 Grease the pie dish with oil, line with pastry and scatter with a third of the hard cheese.

4 In a large bowl mix together the tomatoes, pumpkin, potatoes, zucchini (courgettes), onion, garlic, olives, thyme, bread crumbs, remaining hard cheese and olive oil and season with salt and pepper.

5 Spoon the filling into the pie dish and scatter with crumbled feta.

6 Moisten the edge of the pastry case, place the lid on top and press to seal.

7 Top the pastry with the mozzarella slices and bake for around 40 minutes, covering with foil if it browns too quickly.

8 Remove from the oven, cut into slices, scatter with parsley and serve with lettuce leaves.

CHICK PEA FRITTERS

Ingredients

1 stale bread roll, soaked in water

400 g / 2 cups canned chick peas, rinsed and drained

1 onion, peeled and finely chopped

1 garlic clove, peeled and finely chopped

2 tbsp freshly chopped cilantro (fresh coriander)

½ tsp ground coriander

½ tsp ground cumin

¼ tsp baking powder

1 egg

Bread crumbs

Vegetable oil, for frying

Salt and freshly ground pepper

Method

Prep and cook time: 30 min

1 Squeeze the bread roll well to remove excess liquid.

2 Purée the chick peas with the bread roll, onions and garlic in a mixer.

3 Mix in the cilantro (coriander leaves), ground coriander, cumin, baking powder and egg, adding breadcrumbs if the dough is too moist. Season with salt and pepper.

4 Heat the oil in a skillet and drop in spoonfuls of the mixture, flattening slightly. Fry on each side for 2–3 minutes until golden brown.

SPINACH LASAGNA

Ingredients

1 kg / 2¼ lb fresh spinach

225 g / ½ lb lasagna sheets

1 onion, peeled and finely chopped

2 garlic cloves, peeled and finely chopped

1 tbsp butter, plus extra for greasing

Nutmeg

200 g / 1 cup cream cheese

150 ml / ⅔ cup crème fraîche

60 g / ½ cup grated Emmental cheese

Salt and freshly ground pepper

Method

Prep and cook time: 1 hour 10 min

1 Preheat the oven to 200C (400F / Gas Mark 6).

2 Blanch the spinach briefly in salted water, reserving a few leaves for the garnish. Drain, refresh, squeeze to remove any excess liquid and chop roughly.

3 Soak the lasagna sheets in plenty of cold water for about 10 minutes (place the sheets in one by one to prevent them sticking together).

4 Fry the onion and garlic in butter, add the spinach, remove from the heat and season with salt, pepper and nutmeg.

5 To make the cheese sauce, melt the cream cheese and crème fraîche in a heavy saucepan and season with salt and pepper.

6 Layer up the lasagna sheets, cheese sauce and spinach alternately in a buttered ovenproof dish, finishing with cheese sauce. Scatter with grated Emmental.

7 Bake for about 40 minutes until golden brown (cover with foil if it colors too quickly) and serve garnished with the reserved spinach leaves.

EGGPLANT AND FETA SALAD

Ingredients

4 eggplants (aubergines), chopped into large chunks

6 tbsp olive oil

2 garlic cloves, finely chopped

12 cherry tomatoes

1 tbsp balsamic vinegar

2 tbsp white wine vinegar

150 g / 1 cup feta cheese, roughly crumbled

Salt and freshly ground pepper

Basil, to garnish

Method

Prep and cook time: 40

1 Preheat the oven to 200C (400F / Gas Mark 6).

2 Fry the eggplant (aubergine) chunks on all sides in 3 tbsp of very hot olive oil until colored (about 10 minutes).

3 Add the garlic and fry briefly, season with salt and pepper, remove from the heat and let cool slightly.

4 Brush the tomatoes with about 1 tbsp of oil, place in an ovenproof dish and bake for about 15 minutes in the preheated oven.

5 Whisk together the vinegars and remaining oil, season with salt and pepper and toss with the eggplant.

6 To serve, arrange the eggplant on plates, scatter with feta cheese, top with the tomatoes and garnish with basil.

TOMATO AND BASIL TART

Ingredients

For 1 baking pan about 20 x 20 cm
/ 8 x 8 inches

400 g / 2 cups ricotta cheese

2 eggs

100 ml / 7 tbsp milk

60 g / $2/3$ cup freshly grated
hard cheese

4 sprigs fresh basil, leaves plucked

2 tbsp pine nuts

1 garlic clove

Olive oil

300 g / 12 oz filo pastry

450 g / 1 lb cherry tomatoes, halved

1 tsp brown sugar

2 tbsp lemon juice

Salt and freshly ground pepper

Method

Prep and cook time: 1hour 10 min

1 Preheat the oven to 220C (425F / Gas Mark 7).

2 Mix together the ricotta, eggs, milk and hard cheese and season with salt and pepper.

3 Purée two thirds of the basil leaves to a paste with the pine nuts, garlic and about 5 tbsp olive oil.

4 Grease a baking pan with oil and line with several layers of filo pastry.

5 Spread the pastry base with about two thirds of the pesto and then spread the cheese mixture on top.

6 Toss the tomatoes with the sugar and lemon juice and season with salt and pepper.

7 Arrange the tomatoes on top of the cheese mixture, dot with the remaining pesto and drizzle with a little olive oil.

8 Bake for 35–40 minutes until golden brown. Scatter with the remaining basil leaves 5 minutes before the end of baking time.

9 Remove from the baking pan, cool on a wire rack and serve either warm or cold cut into slices.

Published by Transatlantic Press

First published in 2011

Transatlantic Press
38 Copthorne Road, Croxley Green, Hertfordshire WD3 4AQ

© Transatlantic Press

Images and Recipes by StockFood © The Food Image Agency

Recipes selected by Rene Chan, StockFood

All rights reserved.

No part of this publication may be reproduced or transmitted in any form or by any means,
electronic or mechanical, including photocopying, recording,or any information storage and retrieval system,
without permission in writing from the copyright holders.

A catalogue record for this book is available from the British Library.

ISBN 978–1–907176–51–7

Printed in China